Exploring Mars

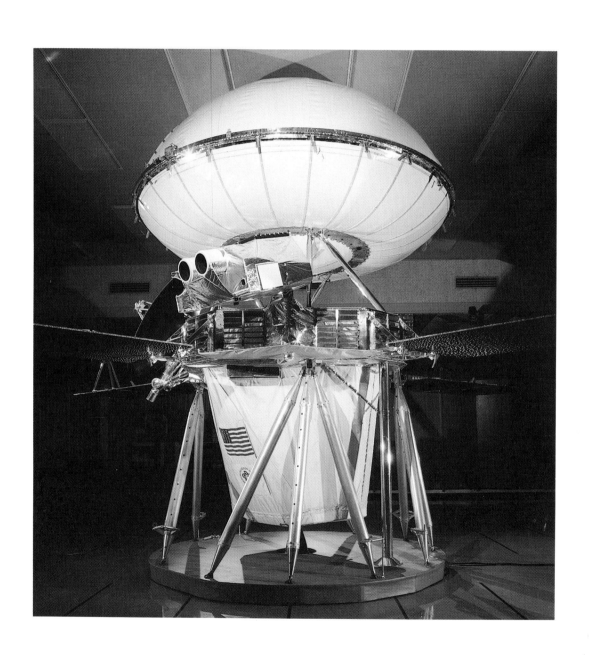

Today's World in Space

Exploring Mars

By David Baker

Rourke Enterprises, Inc.
Vero Beach, FL 32964

Library of Congress Cataloging-in-Publication Data

Baker, David, 1944-
  Exploring Mars / David L. Baker.

  p. cm. — (Today's world in space)
  Bibliography: p.
  Includes index.
  Summary: Discusses the exploration of Mars, focusing on the space flights made by unmanned probes, and examines possible developments and further exploration in the future.
  1. Mars (Planet)—Exploration—Juvenile literature. [1. Space flight to Mars. 2. Mars (Planet) —Exploration.] I. Title. II. Series: Baker, David, 1944- Today's world in space.
QB641.B227 1987   919.9'2304--dc19   87-19889
ISBN 0-86592-404-X   CIP
                                        AC

C.1

CONTENTS

Early Observers

Because it appears reddish-brown when seen through even a small telescope, Mars has long been known as the Red Planet. In 1609 Galileo built the first known telescope. Soon telescopes were being used to search for objects in the *solar system* and features on planets.

The solar system is made up of the sun and nine planets, and all but Mercury and Venus have one or more moons. Markings on Mars were first observed in 1646 by the Italian astronomer Francesco Fontana of Naples. Over the next 300 years, astronomers in several countries turned their telescopes on the Red Planet. As they discovered features on Mars they gave them names in Latin, the language of early science. Areas like Syrtis major, Mare Australe, and Hesperia became commonly recognized.

Science fiction writers have used Mars as the mythical home of intelligent beings, where people farm the land and grow food. Visions of lush, verdant, pasture-supporting growth of different crops appealed to those who believed man was not alone in the solar system. Then visions seemed to be confirmed by telescope views of dark patches appearing in the spring, intensifying in the summer, and disappearing in the winter. Moreover, in 1863, Giovanni Schiaparelli made a drawing of what he thought he had seen through his telescope and proclaimed that Martian beings were constructing canals. He thought water was being routed as *irrigation* for arid deserts making them fertile for summer crops.

For years people dreamed of Mars as a place where they could live and as a planet that would support living things. Even with the best telescope on Earth, astronomers were denied the kind of view seen here until 1964, when spacecraft began to make trips to Mars.

While debate continued as to the possibility of such a dramatic interpretation, scientists were busy establishing some of Mars's basic characteristics. Mars circles the sun in an orbit an average distance of 141.5 million miles and takes 687 earth days to go around the sun one time. Earth orbits at a distance of 93 million miles and takes 365 days to orbit the sun once. Mars takes nearly twice the time, because it is so much farther away and has a greater distance to travel.

With a diameter of 4,240 miles, Mars is little more than half as large as Earth, whose diameter is 7,920 miles. A day on Mars is close to an earth day in length because the Red Planet takes 24 hours and 37 minutes to make one complete *revolution.* That is only 41 minutes longer than the earth takes.

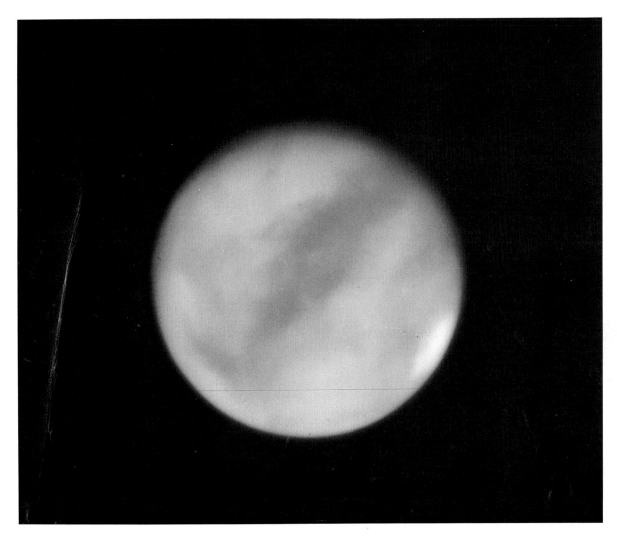

This telescope view of Mars shows how limited the view from Earth was. It led to confusion over many of the surface features and speculation as to whether intelligent beings populated the surface.

Visiting The Red Planet

They learned some information about the planet, but not enough to know if life existed on its surface. By the early 1960s, scientists still believed there was a strong possibility of life on the Red Planet. They thought the pressure of the atmosphere was about one-tenth of Earth's sea-

Until scientists and astronomers could use rockets to send robot spacecraft to Mars, they had to be content with observing the planet from a distance through powerful telescopes.

For a long time it has been known that Mars has two moons, Phobos and Deimos. This artist's view from the surface of Deimos shows Mars as it might look from a distance of 14,600 miles.

Space probes revealed Mars to be quite unlike the hospitable planet everyone expected. This artist's rendition comes close to what Mars must look like from the surface, with dust, canyons, and rocks. The artist assumed that Mars had a blue sky, but space photos have shown it to be red.

level atmospheric pressure, which is 14 pounds for every square inch. In other words, they thought Mars had an atmospheric pressure of 1.4 pound per square inch. That would be enough to support water and, quite possibly, primitive life.

Some astonomers thought Mars has polar caps with frozen water, like the North and South Poles on Earth, forming great sheets of ice. A few scientists even thought the large areas of dark that seemed to creep toward the *equator* in spring were vast expanses of vegetation, although nobody by now seriously believed that intelligent life was digging irrigation canals! Yet, for all that, no one really knew for sure. All in all, Mars would be a fascinating planet to visit and one prime for exploration.

The first United States satellite, *Explorer 1,* was launched on January 31, 1958. It marked the beginning of the space age and followed by less than four months the launch of Russia's *Sputnik 1* on October 4, 1957. Engineers began

to design robot spacecraft to carry instruments built by scientists seeking answers to puzzling questions. The first method they used was *remote sensing.* That is, scientists sent a spacecraft to fly close to Mars, pointing at it a special platform carrying cameras and other sensors.

These instruments would collect information about the planet's temperature, the gases that made up its atmosphere, the density of that atmosphere, and the appearance of its surface features. That last piece of information would be the most dramatic because it would be obtained from television pictures beamed direct to the Earth from the speeding spacecraft. For the first time, it would be like observing the surface from a distance of only a few thousand miles instead of the minimum distance of 35 million miles that seperates Earth from Mars. A high-speed *fly-by* was not quite as exciting as landing on the surface, but it was the best scientists could manage for some years.

Mariner 4 was the first successful spacecraft to fly near Mars on a mission that enabled it to study the planet from a distance.

In record time, NASA, the United States civilian space agency, put together two spacecraft to fly to Mars. Each would be launched by a military missile carrying an additional rocket stage, called Agena, on top. Mariner, as the spacecraft was named, would sit on top of the upper stage and be protected during launch by a shroud. Jettisoned outside the atmosphere, the shroud would fall away to expose the spacecraft which, after the Agena stage fired to put Mariner on course, would separate from the rocket. Weighing a mere 575 pounds, Mariner was to coast along without rocket power like a tiny planet of the sun.

Following a great sweeping circle that carried it to just beyond the orbit of Mars, Mariner's course would coincide with the position of the Red Planet. Pulled slightly out of its original path by the gravity of Mars, the spacecraft would fly within about 6,000 miles of the surface. In a period of less than one hour it would gather more information than scientists had put together form over 300 years of watching the planet through telescopes.

Two spacecraft were prepared, but the first, *Mariner 3,* failed to shed its shroud after launch on November 5, 1964. *Mariner 4* was successfully sent on its way with a launch on November 28, and nearly eight months later it arrived at Mars. What it sent back was a bitter disappointment. Instead of lush greenery and vegetation, all the cameras saw were craters and moon-like features unlike anything expected. Some scientists had hinted they might see craters, but none expected the barren, lifeless world that appeared in the 21 fuzzy black and white pictures from *Mariner 4.* Moreover, instead of an atmosphere one-tenth as dense as Earth, instruments appeared to reveal an atmosphere of poisonous carbon dioxide only one-hundredth as dense as the atmosphere on Earth. It was an atmosphere far too thin to support running water.

The Mariner spacecraft had four large solar panels and scientific instruments for looking at the surface as it flew by at great speed. Note the four veins, one on each solar panel, designed to compensate for pressure from the sun's radiation.

Mapping the Surface

Many parts of the spacecraft were tested under special conditions, simulating the harsh environment they would encounter during the long flight from Earth to Mars.

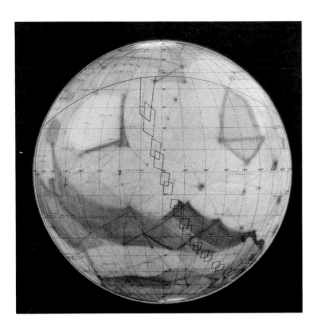

Because *Mariner 4* would fly past Mars at great speed, it had little time to take pictures. This map shows the sequence of 21 views it took during its rapid fly-by.

Sending *Mariner 4* to Mars in 1964 was just one of NASA's several projects aimed at finding out if life existed on the surface of the Red Planet. In fact, the Mariner program had begun with the flights of *Mariner 1* and *Mariner 2* in 1962. Designed to fly by the planet Venus, closer to the sun than Earth, *Mariner 1* was intentionally blown up when it veered off course shortly after launch. *Mariner 2* was a success and became the first spacecraft to send back details from the vicinity of another planet. Mariner spacecraft were standard design, almost like a production line spacecraft, capable of carrying experiments on fly-by missions to the planets. Each Mariner carried instruments appropriate to the planet it was sent to inspect.

To explore Mars more fully, NASA wanted to build a bigger spacecraft capable of going into orbit around that planet. From there, after the orbiter had thoroughly mapped the planet, a landing craft would descend to take samples from the surface. Only then could the question of life be solved. Or so the scientists hoped. Before that, however, two more missions would be sent to survey Mars and begin the process of mapping the features first identified in pictures taken through telescopes and the 21 fuzzy images from *Mariner 4*. It would take a long time to build the surface-sampler, and NASA wanted to know what to expect when the robot finally got there.

The two missions sent to explore further the Red Planet were launched 26 months apart. For each mission, a time was chosen when the relative position of Earth and Mars permitted the best flight path. These flight paths were huge circles, or orbits, of the sun aligned so accurately that they would intersect Mars as it was orbiting the sun. Launches can only take place when the planets are in the correct position. These unique opportunities are called *launch windows,* because they allow the spacecraft to fly with the least amount of rocket power. Launch windows to Mars vary with time but are typically about 25 months apart.

After the first mission to Mars in 1964, NASA chose to improve the basic Mariner and give it more experiments. *Mariner 6* and *Mariner 7,* the second Mars mission, were scheduled for launch in 1969. The first spacecraft was sent on its way

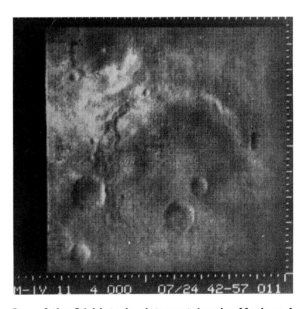

One of the 21 historic pictures taken by *Mariner 4* when it flew past Mars on July 14, 1965. This view was taken from a distance of 7,800 miles and covers an area about 150 miles by 170 miles.

Based on the findings of *Mariner 4*, NASA launched two Mariner spacecraft to the planet Mars in 1969. *Mariner 6* and *Mariner 7* were heavier than their predecessor and carried a bigger load of scientific instruments, most of which can be seen grouped on the platform hinged down at the bottom.

on February 24, and the second on March 27. Each Mariner weighed about 847 pounds and carried two TV cameras. When they flew by Mars in late July and early August, they sent back a total of 210 photographs. These were clearer than the pictures from *Mariner 4*. The planet appeared to be more interesting than had been thought after the first fly-by four years earlier. The photographs confirmed the presence of polar ice caps, although no one could tell if it was frozen water. From the evidence of the second Mars mission, it might have been frozen carbon dioxide.

This mission did little to restore hope for a planet teeming with life. It did, however, pose more questions than it answered. Scientists were getting used to thinking of Mars in a very different way. The space projects had overturned all their earlier theories. It would be up to the next mission, *Mariner 9*, to study the planet for a longer period of time than the brief fly-bys of the two missions to date. *Mariner 9* would pave the way for the first landers, then being planned as one of NASA's most ambitious programs.

Previous missions had sent back pictures of Mars during a brief period when the cameras pointed down at the surface. Other scientific instruments had only a few minutes to record their data as the spacecraft sped on its way. What was needed was an orbiter to keep circling Mars for a long period of time. In that way, cameras and instruments could watch the planet at various times during its day and in different seasons. Only then could scientists understand the way surface features changed with time. There was still the question of the canals. If no life existed, what were the waves of darkening that seemed to grow south from the north polar ice cap? Many questions remained.

NASA launched *Mariner 8*, the first of two planned orbiters, on May 8, 1971. The launching rocket failed and it fell into the sea. The second spacecraft, *Mariner 9*, was more fortunate. It was sent up on May 30 and began a flight lasting just over five months. The spacecraft was by far the heaviest Mariner ever

Together, *Mariner 6* and *Mariner 7* took many more pictures than *Mariner 4*. This view shows a series of overlapping pictures pieced together to give scientists a view of the surface across a wide region. The total area covered here is about 2,500 miles long and 450 miles wide, just a little longer than the distance between Los Angeles and Washington, DC.

launched. It weighed 2,273 pounds at launch, compared with 847 pounds each for *Mariner 6* and *Mariner 7*. *Mariner 4* had weighed just 575 pounds. Much of the extra weight was created by carrying propellant for a main rocket motor. This motor would be used to slow the spacecraft down and put it in a precise orbit around Mars just as it reached its closest approach. Without the motor firing, *Mariner 9* would speed on past the planet, just as the others had. The propellant to carry out the firing weighed 1,050 pounds.

Mariner 9 arrived at Mars on November 13, 1971. Its motor fired for about fifteen minutes, slowing the spacercraft by nearly 3,600 MPH. *Mariner 9* was put into an elliptical orbit which took it to within 869 miles of the surface at the low point and about 26,000 miles at the high

Sent to Mars in 1971, *Mariner 9* was one of two spacecraft designed to orbit the planet and send back a detailed series of pictures for several months. This artist's illustration shows how the two spacecraft would have occupied slightly different elliptical orbits. One spacecraft failed during launch, leaving only one spacecraft to carry out the mission.

point. The time it takes to make one full revolution of a planet is called the *oribital period*. The orbital period for *Mariner 9* was about 11 hours and 58 minutes, a little short of a half day for Mars. This orbital period enabled the cameras to take views of both sides of the planet when they were facing the sun. On each orbit, the path was

Mariner 9 was a developed version of the previous Mariners sent to Mars, with very large fuel tanks. It also had a rocket motor for reducing the speed of the spacecraft as it neared the planet, so it could drop into an elliptical path. Note the white heat protective blanket over the fuel tanks with the engine nozzle facing upward at the top. Just beyond the nozzle, appearing to lie over it, is a scientific probe on the other side of the spacecraft.

a little to one side of the previous path, allowing Mariner 9 to map the whole planet every 20 days. By continually watching the same areas over many months, seasonal changes could be followed.

When *Mariner 9* first got into orbit, Mars was experiencing one of the worst dust storms on record. Unlike anything on earth, dust storms on Mars whip up fine sandy particles into great clouds reaching several miles into the air. They are caused by changes in the atmosphere and go through predictable cycles. It was unfortunate that just when Mariner 9 reached Mars, the cameras were unable to see anything. The dust

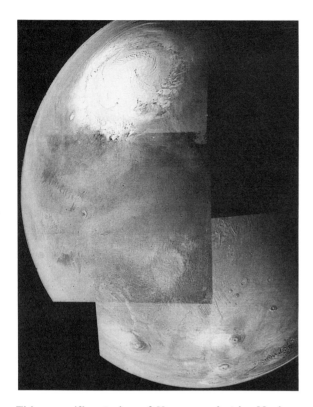

This magnificent view of Mars was shot by *Mariner 9* on August 7, 1972, assembled from a series of several pictures made up to form a mosaic. The three pictures were among 7,273 obtained by *Mariner 9*, taken 84 seconds apart from a distance of 8,500 miles.

south of the planet's equator, and what looked like dried-up river beds were seen in the north.

As the weeks and months rolled by, Mars began to fascinate scientists more and more. It was as though they had gotten over their disappointment at not finding evidence of vegetation. What they saw now might not be as exciting as visible forms of life, but it was not as dead a world as the moon was known to be. Could water have flowed across the surface millions of years ago, making seas and oceans from deserts and barren plains? No one could say, but the signs were there.

Several times *Mariner 9*'s orbit was changed by firing up the rocket motor for a few seconds. This enabled it to take better pictures of interesting sites on the surface. When its mission finally ended on October 27, 1972, *Mariner 9*

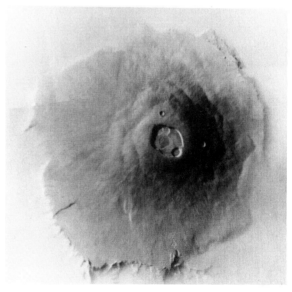

This remarkable view of Olympus Mons was taken when the dust of the great Martian sandstorm subsided in late January, 1972. It shows what is now known to be the biggest volcano on any planet in the solar system, 372 miles across at the base with cliffs 10,000 feet high and a main crater 40 miles across, standing 14 miles above the surrounding terrain.

rose high into the air, reaching almost 20 miles above the surface. Gradually, over a period of weeks, the wind dropped and the dust began to settle. What the cameras saw then was contrary to anything anyone had anticipated.

The previous mission to Mars had done little to help answer questions about some of the big features seen through telescopes from Earth. As the dust began to settle, the cameras aboard *Mariner 9* peered through the murk. They took pictures of the tops of giant volcanoes higher than any on Earth. Great canyons came into view, far bigger than any seen before. Wild, hilly patches of land looked like the Arizona desert, and badlands with rolling sand dunes appeared. Large craters littered the surface, particularly

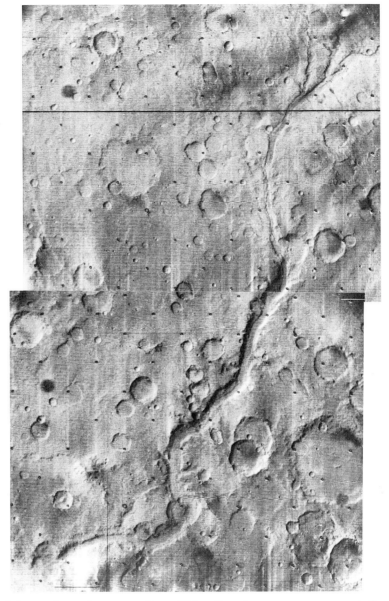

This picture of a sinuous valley 435 miles long was composed from two photographs taken by *Mariner 9* on January 22, 1972. It shows what may have been the result of flowing water at some early point in the history of Mars.

had been operating in orbit for just over half a Martian year. It had seen seasonal changes that helped explain the strange wave of darkening at springtime. It was not vegetation cultivated by intelligent life, but merely the movement of volcanic ash across the surface caused by high winds at that time of the year. Lifeless, *Mariner 9* will continue to orbit Mars for more than 50 years before crashing to the surface.

In all, *Mariner 9* shot more than 7,300

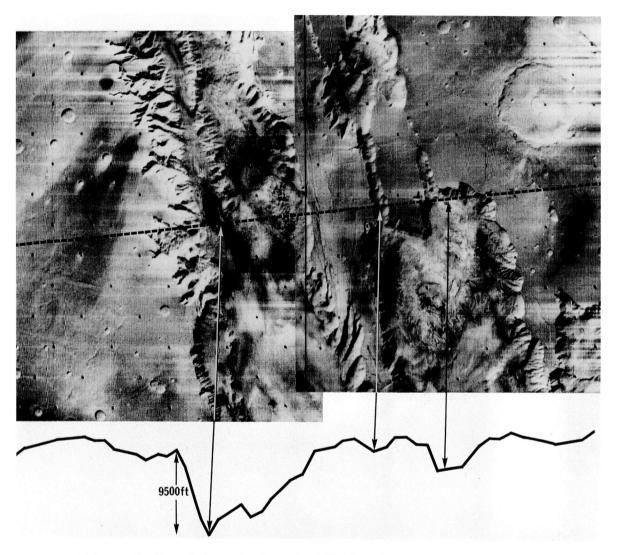

9500 ft

This mosaic of two photographs shows the 9,500-foot deep canyon known as Valles Marineris. The approximate contours of the canyon can be seen at the bottom. This canyon is 75 miles across and is seen here in photographs taken from an altitude of 1,070 miles covering an area 400 miles square.

photographs including views of the two potato-shaped moons, Phobos and Deimos. They are tiny worlds, not much more than big lumps of rock. Phobos is about 13 miles by 17 miles, while Deimos is less than half that size. *Mariner* 9 did something else very useful. It more accurately measured the atmosphere of Mars. Information like this was essential in assuming the success of the big lander project, Viking. Like a capsule falling to Earth, the lander would use the atmosphere to help brake it's fall to the surface of Mars. What the atmosphere was made of and how dense it was were vital pieces of information for engineers if they were to build the right sort of lander shield.

Flying by Mars, and even mapping it from orbit, were not sufficient to satisfy scientists. They still wanted to know if life existed on the Red Planet. No one now expected animal life, but few thought it was a completely dead world. For years, biologists had been working with NASA engineers to build instruments to send to Mars. Their work was made difficult by the distance involved. Separated by tens of millions of miles, biologists would have to work through computers to send instructions to the Viking lander. It takes a radio signal around 20 minutes to reach a space craft on Mars and another 20 minutes for the answer to come back. Viking would have to be a very special kind of robot.

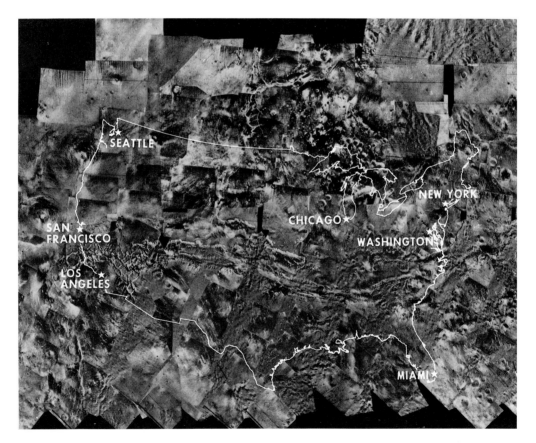

The Valles Marineris canyon complex is vast by any scale and stretches across a greater distance than that separating the Atlantic Ocean from the Pacific Ocean across the continental United States.

Vikings on Mars

Right: This insignia was designed and painted as the emblem of the Viking mission to Mars. The astronomical symbol for Mars encompasses the earth, alluding to the fascination the Red Planet has had on the mind of man for centuries. The arrowhead points to the prime landing site for the first Viking mission.

Below: The Viking spacecraft included an orbiter and a lander. Here, the lander is seen being attached to its shield, which will protect it while it coasts to Mars attached to the orbiter. The three landing legs can be seen folded up, and the two vertical TV cameras look like posts to the right of the spacecraft's center line.

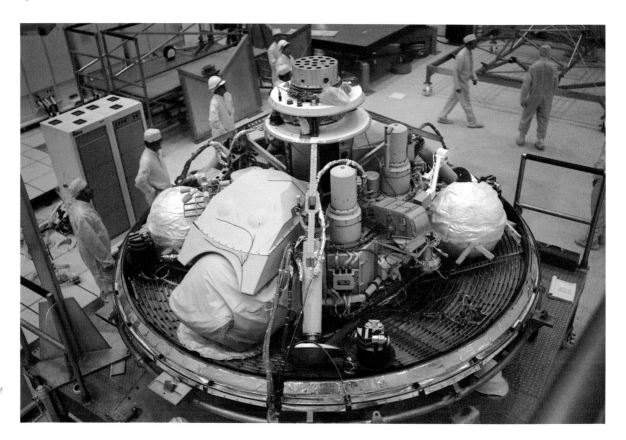

The Viking lander is encapsulated, where it will remain sterilized so as not to contaminate the environment of Mars. There is international agreement on the sterilization of spacecraft to prevent pollution of what could be a primitive form of life.

Scientists and engineers at NASA's Jet Propulsion Laboratory (JPL) in Pasadena, California, and at the Langley Research Center in Virginia, labored for more than ten years to put working robots on the surface of Mars. They had help from industry, in particular from Martin Marietta, the Denver-based aerospace company that built the lander and most of the launch vehicle that would send Viking on its way. NASA gathered together many scientists from the United States and other countries around the world. Each would contribute, helping to design the many different instruments carried by Viking to the surface.

Two Viking spacecraft would be launched several weeks apart during a launch window that opened in mid-August, 1975. Each Viking was two spacecraft connected together, an orbiter and a lander. The orbiter weighed 5,138 pounds, more than twice the weight of the previous orbiter, *Mariner 9.* The lander weighed 2,646 pounds. Some of that weight was a protective shell that covered the spacecraft until it began its landing operations.

The Viking orbiter was big. When unfolded to convert sunlight into electricity, its solar panels were 32 feet across. They provided 800 watts of energy to power the spacecraft. By comparison, the first Mars explorer, *Mariner 4,* produced just 195 watts! The orbiter carried 3,153 pounds of propellant, some of which would be used to place it in orbit around Mars. The orbiter would have to carry the lander inside its protective shell all the way to Mars, and place them both into an elliptical orbit of the planet.

Before releasing the lander, the orbiter would send TV pictures back to Earth. The pictures would help scientists find the best spot to put the lander on. After the lander touched down, the Viking orbiter would pick up signals from it and send them back to Earth. In this way the orbiter was similar to a small relay station. The orbiter would continue to map the surface while the lander operated from the surface far below.

A very special spacecraft, the Viking lander was carried to the orbit of Mars inside a protective cocoon attached to the orbiter by struts. On the surface, the lander received electricity from

Completely assembled, the Viking orbiter at bottom supports the lander and its aeroshell on top. Note the two Viking orbiter cameras which peer like round eyes to the left of the main structure. The lower white section shrouds the fuel tanks required to reduce speed for the complete assembly to enter Mars orbit.

two nuclear power plants that produced heat from radioactive decay of plutonium. The lander had three legs, so it could remain stable on uneven surfaces within a circle 9 feet in diameter. Two color TV cameras rested on top of the main hexgonal body and a weather mast measured temperature, wind speed, and wind direction. Other instruments measured composition of the atmosphere and its pressure.

To help detect Marsquakes, should there be

any, each lander had a seismometer to measure vibrations through the surface. Each lander also had a mechanical arm attached to the side of the spacecraft extending 10 feet across the surface with a tiny scoop at one end. The sampler could dig trenches, strike the surface, and measure the hardness of the soil. When delivering samples to a special windproof hopper for the biology experiments, the arm would turn its scoop over and shake tiny particles through a small sieve, leaving stones in the scoop's cup-like handle.

Of the four biology instruments inside the lander body, three were connected by a tiny conveyor belt. One looked for photosynthesis, a process where plants grow by turning carbon dioxide into matter and giving out oxygen. Earth gets most of its oxygen from plants in this way. Another instrument looked for signs of *organisms* that take food from the atmosphere. The third looked for life by watching for changes in the gases of a sealed container to which samples of soil were sent by a conveyor. All living things give off gases as they consume food. The fourth biology experiment had a special hopper of its own and looked for life by heating samples and measuring the gases given off for signs of organic molecules, the remnants of living things.

Because of the time needed for radio signals to travel between Earth and Mars, both orbiter and lander had to have powerful computers. In these would be stored detailed information, so that each spacecraft could be programmed to

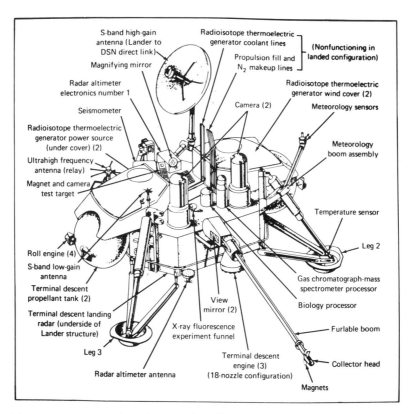

The Viking lander was a functional scientific research station carrying many experiments and complex items of equipment. In addition, Viking contained the systems necessary to keep the spacecraft running and operating in good condition on the surface of this alien world.

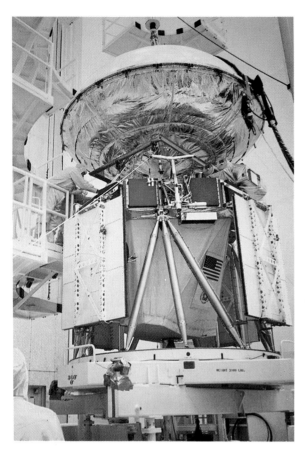

Ready for flight, a Viking spacecraft, orbiter, and lander is assembled on the launch vehicle at Cape Canaveral in Florida.

operate for many hours without further instruction. A complete sequence of movements necessary to move the lander's mechanical arm out and have it grab a small rock required several hundred different instructions.

The rocket that sent each Viking spacecraft on its way had to lift the combined weight of the orbiter and lander. With a total weight of nearly 4 tons, each Viking was more than three times the weight of the *Mariner 9* probe and almost fourteen times the weight of *Mariner 4*. The rocket, Titan Centaur, stood 159 feet tall and at

Right: Launched in August, 1975, on the most powerful rocket in operational service with the United States space program in that year, a Titan IIIE-Centaur lifts off smoothly to begin the historic mission.

liftoff had a thrust of more than 2 million pounds. This thrust was more than five times that of the Atlas Centaur, which launched the Mariners.

The first Viking was launched from Cape Canaveral during the late afternoon of August 20, 1975. It was followed by the second Viking on September 9, 1975. For several months, engineers on Earth sent radio commands to the spacecraft and received signals back about their condition. With each passing month the Vikings drew closer to Mars, drifting through a great big circle toward the Red Planet.

The first to arrive, the *Viking 1* orbiter engine fired for 38 minutes on June 19, 1976. It burned off more that 2,300 pounds of fuel, slowing the orbiter and its lander by 2,460 MPH. That put it in an elliptical orbit around Mars. A few hours later the orbit was changed by a further firing of the main engine. *Viking 1* was now in a path that carried it to within 940 miles of the surface and out to a maximum distance of 20,257 miles. *Viking 1* would take one Mars day to make one full orbit of the Red Planet, passing at the same time each day over the spot scientists had picked for the landing.

The Viking orbiter TV cameras sent detailed pictures back to Earth. Along with radar scans showing the roughness of the surface, these photographs indicated rocks and boulders that might topple the lander when it descended. Engineers commanded the Viking orbiter to fire its engine and drift slowly across the planet so scientists could select a safer landing site. They

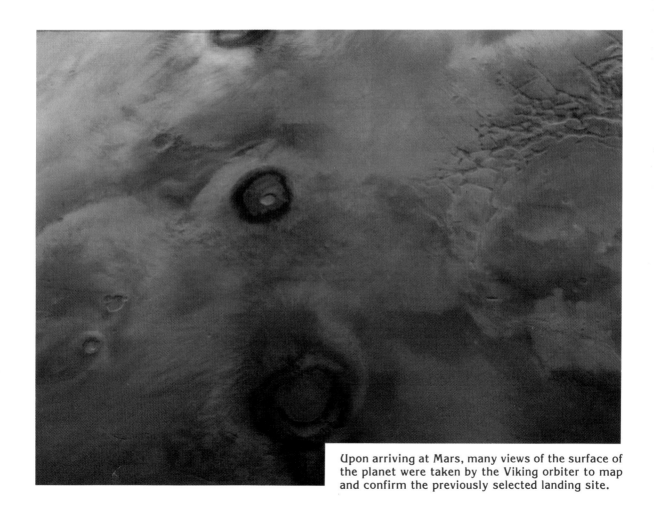

Upon arriving at Mars, many views of the surface of the planet were taken by the Viking orbiter to map and confirm the previously selected landing site.

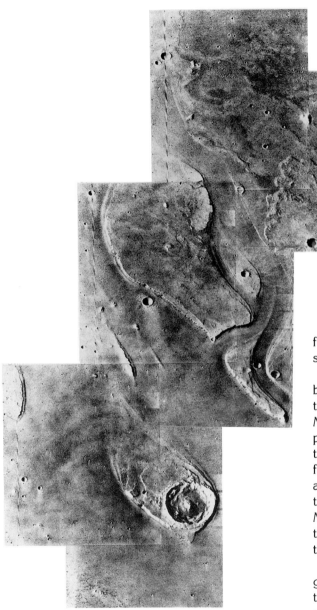

Pictures like these, while of great scientific interest for the evidence they might produce about the possibility of flowing water long ago, also provided information which helped engineers to re-plan the precise landing spot.

found one, and on July 20, 1976, the lander was separated from the orbiter to begin the descent.

Fixed inside a dish-shaped aeroshell, the braking effect of the thin atmosphere reduced the lander's speed from 10,300 MPH to 670 MPH. The aeroshell was released and a parachute came out, slowing the lander to less than 140 MPH. Just 4,000 feet above the surface, three landing rockets ignited. Throttled by a computer getting data from a landing radar, the motors slowed the speed of descent to just 5 MPH, at which point the *Viking 1* lander dug its three footpads into the red soil at a place called the Golden Plains.

On Mars it was late afternoon, and the sun was going down. Within minutes the first TV pictures came back. Rocks, boulders, sand dunes, and gently rolling hills were seen for the first time from the surface of the Red Planet. The sky was a gentle pink, and the dust and soil a rust-colored red. Scientists discovered that the atmosphere was 3 percent nitrogen and confirmed that it was mostly carbon dioxide. As it continued to map the planet, the orbiter up above determined that the polar caps were probably

When the Viking landers reached the surface of Mars, they revealed a desolate world populated with many rocks, boulders, and dust dunes. Note the pinkish sky, caused by the red rust color of reflected light from the surface.

frozen carbon dioxide, with ice at the north pole.

The second Viking reached its orbit of Mars on August 7, 1976, while *Viking 1* was carrying out its reconnaissance. Lander 2 touched down on the other side of the planet from lander 1 on September 3. Its landing site was a place named Utopia, with many more rocks than the first site. Now there were two spacecraft on the surface and two in orbit, all taking thousands of pictures and measurements.

The search for life began just seven days after lander 1 reached the Golden Plains. Scientists had until early November, 1976, to carry out their tests with the biology instruments. At that time the relative position of the sun, Earth and Mars would prevent communications for about five weeks. The Vikings had been built to operate for 90 days. There was no guarantee they would be operating in mid-December when Mars moved around from behind the sun.

When all the tests had been carried out, the biology experiments seemed to indicate the existence of a very simple form of life on the planet. There was no positive evidence, however. No organisms could be identified. Scientists were puzzled and remain so today. They saw signs that on Earth would be interpreted as living matter, but there were no dead bodies of tiny microbes. More tests were conducted when the two Viking landers resumed operations in December, 1976. They had survived and continued to work for a long time.

Viking 2 was the first to stop operating. In July, 1978, The orbiter ran out of fuel for its attitude control jets, the tiny thrusters that kept its

The Viking lander had two cameras to monitor operations at the surface. It also had a long extended arm which could dig and scrape the surface in addition to collecting material to deliver to hoppers on top of the spacecraft, feeding instruments searching for life.

The communications antenna and the top of the spacecraft is clearly seen here as one of the two stereocolor TV cameras looks back across the Martian terrain.

solar cells pointing to the sun. The lander quit working in April, 1980, having operated on the surface for more than three years. The Viking 1 orbiter ran out of fuel in August, 1980. It had been orbiting the planet for more than four years. Its lander kept going until November, 1982.

The first lander to reach the surface of Mars had been working for more than six years. It failed only because an engineer at mission control sent the wrong command and turned the antenna away from Earth. It could no longer send or receive signals. In all, the Vikings returned more than 54,000 pictures.

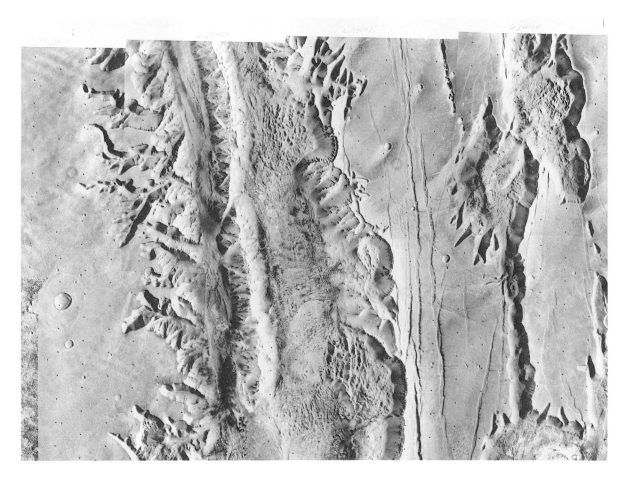

Giant canyons first mapped by *Mariner 9* in 1972 were seen in much greater detail by the Viking orbiter as it ceaselessly continued to orbit the planet, taking pictures and gathering other scientific data.

Human Expeditions

The question about possible life forms on Mars reached hysteric proportions when H.G. Wells envisaged Martian landers invading England, as seen here in an illustration from his historic book, *The War of the Worlds.*

People have wanted to go to Mars for a very long time. Ordinary people as well as scientists and engineers have held on to that dream. Mars is so much farther away than the moon that this dream might seem strange. But it makes sense when the different conditions on the two worlds are considered. The moon is an airless place without any possibility of life, either now or in the past. It is a dead place where little happens. Mars, on the other hand, is capable of supporting life and might even have primitive forms of micro-organisms on it. Mars offers the possibility of exploring a planet not so very different from our own.

What we know today about Mars comes largely from the Mariner fly-by missions, the *Mariner 9* orbiter, and the Viking orbiters and landers. But scientists are far from fully understanding the planet. Many questions remain unanswered, and many more have been posed by the findings of the spacecraft. Even if answers exist to these questions, space missions are expensive. We cannot expect all planets to receive a continuing series of visits.

It has been more than ten years since the last American spacecraft went to Mars. Part of the reason is that scientists have been concentrating on other planets farther away than Mars. Deep-space robots sent to visit them take many years to reach their destinations. However, the time is coming when astronauts will fly to Mars and explore its surface. How will that happen, and what will they do when they get there?

Essential for sustaining a major expedition to the moon and the planets, this reusable spaceplane was designed by rocket engineers in the 1950s. The rocket motor that boosted it into orbit is seen falling away.

Plans to explore Mars have existed since the beginning of the space age in the late 1950s. Before that, people thought that the best way to explore the planets would begin with a reusable shuttle followed by a big wheel-shaped space station. Werner von Braun, the man who designed and built the mighty Saturn rockets that took men to the moon, developed such a plan. He saw the space station as a stepping stone to the moon and Mars.

Von Braun was wrong about the way men would first go into space, but he was right about the importance of a space station. NASA is designing a space station to be assembled in earth orbit during the mid-1990s. It will be a suitable place from which to begin the colonization of the moon and Mars. It takes less rocket power to go to the moon from earth orbit than it does to go from the surface of the earth to a space station only 250 miles up.

When Apollo astronauts went to the moon, the chances that they might bring back bugs were very slim. If there *is* life on Mars, it could mean disease and terrible plagues for Earth if

Changes do occur on the surface of Mars, as shown here by a picture taken May 18, 1979, from the *Viking 2* lander touchdown site. The photo reveals water ice on rocks and soil. Robot spacecraft that return to Earth with samples removed from the surface of Mars may be contaminated and will have to be de-contaminated at an earth-orbiting space station.

those microbes mixed with germs in the atmosphere. A space station would be a suitable place for returning astronauts to stay while scientists tested tham and their samples for signs of living organisms. An epidemic of Martian bugs could prove fatal.

Before humans go to Mars, scientists need more information about the planet itself. So far only two landers have sampled the surface at two sites. The next spacecraft to go there will have to extend that survey. First, a very extensive survey from orbit will continue the mapping work begun by *Mariner 9* and the two Viking orbiters. Then sites for a more sophisticated robot lander will be chosen.

The Viking orbiter cameras were able to see objects down to about 260 feet across. Scientists need to improve the equipment so it will photograph much smaller objects. They would also like to be able to measure accurately the

NASA plans to assemble in the mid-1990s a space station with the capability of serving as a receiving base for samples of moon rock. This would help biologists inspect the samples to see if they carry any harmful organisms.

Next in the sequence of robot spacecraft to visit the Red Planet will be the NASA Mars Observer, to be launched in the early 1990s. This spacecraft will map the surface in great detail, preparing the way for the next planned phase in the exploration of Mars.

height of hills, mountains, volcanoes, and valleys. They plan to do this by sending a radio signal to the ground from a spacecraft in a precisely circular orbit and measuring the time it takes to return. In addition scientists will accurately measure the temperature and the wind conditions to understand processes in the atmosphere that affect the movement of dust and sand.

The next expedition to the Red Planet, the NASA Mars Observer mission, will do all these things. To be launched in September, 1992, the 4,700-pound spacecraft will be sent on its way by the shuttle. A year later it will go into orbit around Mars only 224 miles above the surface and continue to operate for more than a full Mar-

tian year, or two years on Earth. It will be the first of a series of spacecraft aimed at preparing the way for manned landings.

Nobody knows exactly what the next step will be. Almost certain to follow Mars Observer, however, is a sample-return flight. In this flight, a Mars rover would roam across the surface and explore different sites. The rover, which might be about 20 feet long and 6 feet wide, would be made up of three cabs linked together like trucks behind a locomotive. The cabs would have two wheels, each more than 3 feet in diameter. These would allow it to climb over rocks and boulders. The cabs would be linked with flexible ties allowing the rover to snake across the rocky surface.

To explore widely different geographic regions on the surface of Mars, a rover will be essential equipment. This artist's impression shows one concept under study by NASA.

The Mars rover would weigh about 1,500 pounds and carry its own guidance and navigation equipment. Controllers on earth could guide it via TV screens, or it could be programmed to pick its own course. The rover would probably roam about 3,000 feet a day and collect samples to carry back to the landing site. After the samples had been put aboard a return vehicle, the rover would go off on its own again to continue its exploration, sending TV pictures back to earth.

NASA scientists can only guess when such a mission might take place. A typical schedule could begin with launch toward Mars in December, 1998. Arriving at the Red Planet in late 1999, the spacecraft would set the rover down on the surface to begin a long survey of the area. The position of the planets at that time would not permit a return flight to Earth before January, 2001. The rover would have more that a year to gather samples. Under this plan, the samples would arrive back at the space station in November, 2001.

Because launch windows to Mars only come around every 25 months, advance planning is particularly important if opportunities are not to be missed. The timing of the launch windows can also affect the length of time between landing on Mars and taking off. For example, if launched in 1996, the return rocket would have to wait only eleven months before it could take off for Earth. If launched at the end of the year 2000, it would have to wait eighteen months.

Some scientists maintain that the best way to reach Mars is to first put a base on the moon. Before that could happen, orbiters would have to map the moon's surface more accurately than

Apollo did in its six successful missions between 1969 and 1972. Detailed reconnaissance would be carried out by robot rovers like those planned for Mars. In fact, similar vehicles might be suitable for both worlds. Manned flights might then begin by the year 2000, while detailed surveys using robots were under way at Mars.

Between 2005 and 2010 a construction base could begin, with four landings each year to bring supplies and carry out the work. Manned flights to Mars would be considerably more economical if they could use oxygen taken from rocks on the moon. The lunar base would provide the oxygen-processing plant to help power the rocket ships taking men to Mars. Fueled

This artist's illustration depicts a Mars sample-return mission, with the top stage lifting off to return to Earth.

with hydrogen carried up from Earth, the Mars ships could depart the earth-moon system for planet Mars by 2011.

Scientists would want to set up a base on Mars as they had on the moon, providing two research stations similar to United States stations in Antarctica. They would use them as base camps and travel far across the surface in vehicles developed from the unmanned rover program of the 1990s. Teams of up to four people could travel several days at a time, living in the vehicle and using it to carry rock and soil samples.

Another design for a Mars soil sample-return flight might require the vehicle to touch down in one spot and obtain all its samples without using a rover. A combination of a rover mission and a sample-return flight might rendezvous with separate vehicles at the surface of Mars.

Engineers have proposed this simplified lander-rover developed from the Viking program.

Before men set up the first Mars base, many rovers and sample-return missions may have taken place. This particular vehicle is probing rocks some distance away from the lander.

Back at the main camp, greenhouses would provide most of the food, with compressed carbon dioxide from the Martian atmosphere used to help plants produce oxygen. Living quarters would be modules weighing 38,000 pounds each, similar to the type used in NASA's first space station in the mid-1990s. They would be buried under 3 feet of soil to protect people from the sun's radiation. Although Mars is much farther from the sun than the Earth, its atmosphere has no protective screen as ours does.

Launch and landing sites for rockets coming to and from the base would be made from soilbased concrete. Special maintenance facilities would keep all the machinery working, and small nuclear generators would provide all the electrical power. Because many areas on Mars are thought to have water locked up as ice just below the surface, wells would break down this permafrost and provide running water for drinking and washing. Because Mars has one-third the gravity of Earth, there would be no problem taking a shower.

For really distant surveys, explorers would take to the air, flying great distances in small glider-like planes. Using tiny rocket thrusters to take off and land, these Martian *microlights* would be kept in the air by propellers slowly moving them along at about 50 MPH. Scientists would take to the air to map new areas and search for canyons, craters, and ridges to explore. Eventually, people would transfer between the moon and Mars bases, perhaps collecting together on Mars in the year 2019 to celebrate the 50th anniversary of the first manned landing on the moon.

Opposite page: Within the next twenty years, a Mars base like this one may very well become reality.

Why go to Mars?

Above: Great wonders await exploration by robots and human explorers in the next twenty or thirty years. This spectacular view of the top of Olympus Mons, the biggest volcano in the solar system, shows it to be more than 90,000 feet high – about three times the height of Mount Everest!

Mars science contains many valuable lessons for the study of Earth, its history, and its resources. Studying the evolution of distant worlds helps us to understand some of the conditions involved in forming the features on the surface of Earth.

Space flight is expensive. To send men to Mars will cost billions of dollars. So why do it? Robots are cheaper and can do almost the same job of surveying and taking pictures. Would it not be better to spend less money on more un-manned spacecraft like Viking, the rover, and the sample-return vehicle NASA will probably develop for the late 1990s? After all, if the mission fails, no lives will be lost.

These are powerful arguments. For thousands of years, human beings had no option. If they wanted to find out about a place, they had to visit it themselves. In the last 50 years, great progress with electronic devices has given us the choice of sending a robot or going in person. The space program itself is an example of the breakthrough in automation and *robotics*. Some people believe it has given humans the chance to do more dangerous jobs without risk, because they can build machines to carry out their work.

Other people say that the human race has a responsibility to explore the worlds around it. They see it as part of progress; without human exploration we would not make great discoveries necessary to improve our quality of life. Better hospitals, new drugs to help sick people, improved means of travel, and more reliable machines can all result from space exploration. The Apollo moon program has shown this to be true.

It is estimated that the economy of the United States received in return seven times what it paid for Apollo. In other words, for each dollar spent on Apollo, the nation got seven dollars back. This money came from improved exports, higher quality electronics, and better products. Those figures do not take into account other benefits, such as an improved understanding of our own world gained from close examination of the moon.

What might we get back from Mars if we send people there? The moon goal, set by President Kennedy in 1961, forced people to develop rockets and spacecraft that would never have built without that challenge. So too would a Mars mission bring enormous benefits for people everywhere. The technology necessary to run a Mars program would provide rockets and spacecraft to mine valuable minerals.

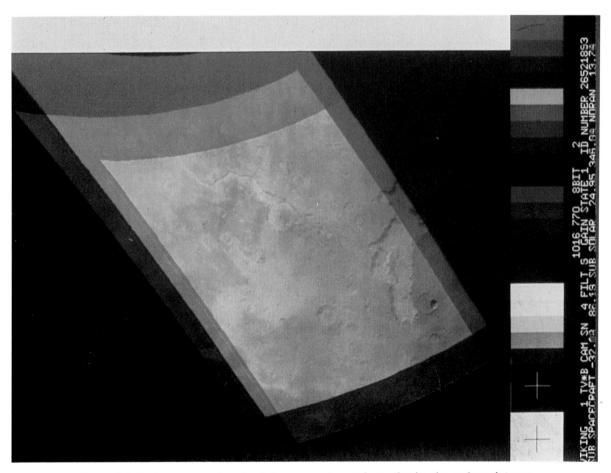

Many detailed and complex techniques were used to obtain the color pictures returned by the Viking orbiter and lander spacecraft. Seen here, different filters overlaid onto a single reproduction provide the color build-up necessary to achieve the correct tone and texture.

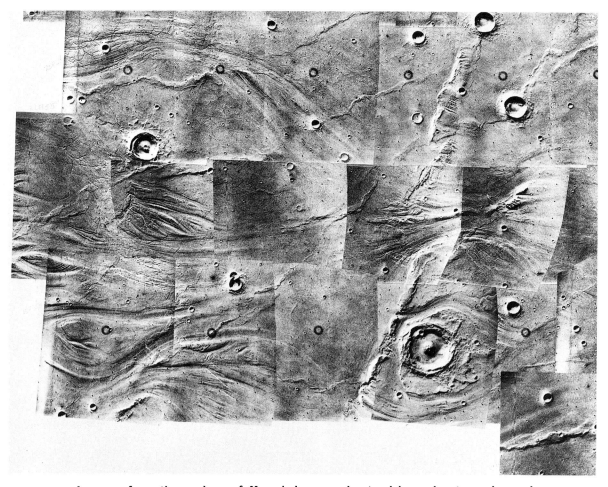

Lessons from the geology of Mars help us understand how planets evolve and change through billions of years. This picture shows detailed evidence of water flows and is similar to sea floor features on Earth.

Earth is running out of important materials that are impossible to produce artificially. These materials are necessary for certain electronic products, such as heart pacemakers and miniature computers. Many of these materials are found on the moon and Mars. With the technology needed to set up a Mars base, we could mine *asteroids,* huge rocks and boulders deep in the solar system containing rare materials. Asteroids could be towed back to the vicinity of Earth and their resources used over many years. Regular trips from the moon and Mars could help replenish diminishing supplies of these minerals on Earth.

Another equally important advantage is harder to measure. By going to the moon, we learned how beautiful our own planet is in the vastness of space. We learned how hostile other worlds are and how precious our own planet is. We also learned how fragile Earth is and how easily the balance of nature can be upset, putting at risk our own lives and those of others. The Apollo program saw the beginning of manned planetary exploration, but it also created concern about the environment and about the delicate balance of nature all over the planet.

By going to Mars, we can improve our understanding of how to care for our earth. Mars seems to be following a sequence not unlike that Earth has been through, although at a much slower pace. There is abundant evidence that water flowed freely on Mars not so long ago and that rivers carved deep gorges between mountains and canyons. We need to understand the processes that caused that to start and then to stop. We may discover important information about the way we are changing the environment of our own planet. If a manned journey to Mars does no more than give us a fresh perspective on our own world, that alone will make it all worthwhile.

Assuming that the present level of effort in the exploration of the solar system is maintained, Mars will probably receive the first human explorers to establish a scientific outpost, similar to those in the Antarctic. These trench marks made by the scoop on the *Viking 1* lander are merely the first in a series of excavations that robot spacecraft will perform between now and the time when human beings set foot on the planet, perhaps as soon as the turn of the century.

GLOSSARY

Aeroshell	A protective shell shaped like a sauce-pan lid, designed to absorb heat built up through friction during entry into the atmosphere of Earth or another planet.
Apollo	The NASA manned spaceflight project of the 1960s and early 1970s devised to land astronauts on the surface of the moon.
Asteroids	Numerous small rocks, boulders, and dust particles that move around the sun between the orbits of Mars and Jupiter.
Astronomer	The scientist who studies astronomy and usually uses telescopes to make observations of objects in space.
Deimos	The smaller of the two moons of Mars and the one farther away from the planet.
Elliptical	Usually a flattened circle or the shape of an orbit similar to the shape of an ellipse.
Equator	The great circle of a planet that divides it into northern and southern hemispheres.
Fly-by	A mission designed to send a spacecraft traveling past another planet so that it can make a reconnaissance or survey of the planet's physical characteristics.
Irrigation	To supply land with water by means of artificial canals, ditches, or pipes to promote the growth of food crops.
Jet Propulsion Laboratory (JPL)	Owned and operated by the California Institute of Technology, JPL operates as the mission control center for most planetary missions and is responsible for project management.
Langley Research Center	The NASA center responsible for having developed the Viking Lander in the early 1970s.
Launch window	The period of time when a spacecraft can be launched, determined by the alignment of planets, for easiest travel of a probe to its destination.
Marsquakes	Disturbances in the planet Mars that create vibrations or rumblings similar to earthquakes on Earth.
Microlite	A hang-glider fitted with a small engine allowing it to take off and land like a small plane.
NASA	National Aeronautics and Space Administration, set up in October, 1958 for the peaceful exploration of space.
Orbit	The curved path, usually almost circular, followed by a planet or satellite in its motion around another body in space.
Orbital period	The time required for a satellite or a planet to make one full orbit.
Organisms	Any living animal or plant, including any bacteria or virus.
Phobos	The larger of the two moons of Mars and the one closer to the planet.

Red Planet	The popular name given to the planet Mars because of its reddish appearance when viewed through a telescope.
Remote Sensing	Measurement and observation of land or the surface of another planet by examining reflected light or other forms of radiation.
Revolution	One complete turn in a circle, or a complete orbit around another body.
Robotics	The science of automated machines programmed to perform mechanical functions in place of a human being.
Solar system	The system containing the sun and the bodies held in its gravitational field including the planets, the asteroids, and comets.

INDEX

Page numbers in *italics* refer to photographs or illustrations.